W9-AJX-130

Siân Owen

This Land

WITHDRAWN

Bloomsbury Methuen Drama
An imprint of Bloomsbury Publishing Plc

B L O O M S B U R Y
LONDON • OXFORD • NEW YORK • NEW DELHI • SYDNEY

Bloomsbury Methuen Drama

An imprint of Bloomsbury Publishing Plc

50 Bedford Square	1385 Broadway
London	New York
WC1B 3DP	NY 10018
UK	USA

www.bloomsbury.com

Bloomsbury is a registered trademark of Bloomsbury Publishing Plc

First published 2016

British Library Cataloguing-in-Publication Data
A catalogue record for this book is available from the British Library

ISBN: PB: 978-1-3500-0138-1
ePub: 978-1-3500-0139-8
ePDF: 978-1-3500-0137-4

Library of Congress Cataloging-in-Publication Data
A catalog record for this book is available from the Library of Congress

Typeset by Country Setting, Kingsdown, Kent CT14 8ES

PENTABUS
RURAL THEATRE COMPANY

SALISBURY
PLAYHOUSE

A Pentabus Theatre Company and
Salisbury Playhouse Production

This Land

by Siân Owen

Supported using public funding by

**ARTS COUNCIL
ENGLAND**

LOTTERY FUNDED

This Land

was first performed at Pentabus, Bromfield,
on 9 March 2016 with the following cast and creative team:

Cast

Rosie Armstrong
Harry Long

Creative Team

Writer	**Siân Owen**
Director	**Jo Newman**
Designer	**Jean Chan**
Lighting Designer	**James Mackenzie**
Sound Designer	**James Frewer**
Technical Stage Manager	**Sam Eccles**
Production Manager	**Tammy Rose**
Set Builder	**Rob Hill**
Design Intern	**Amy Trigg**
PR (Northern Ireland)	**Sarah Hughes, AVA Consulting**

Thanks to

Liz Craven, Manjeet Mann, Ben Addis,
Charlotte Willis, Guy Sanders

Original Drama at Salisbury Playhouse
is sponsored by Frank and Elizabeth Brenan

Tour Dates 2016

9 March	Pentabus, Shropshire
10 March	All Stretton Village Hall, Shropshire
11 March	Snailbeach Village Hall, Shropshire
12 March	SpArC Theatre, Shropshire
16 March	The Talbot Theatre, Whitchurch Leisure Centre, Shropshire
17 March	Foxlowe Arts Centre, Staffordshire
18 March	Ledbury Market Theatre, Herefordshire
19 March	Worcester Arts Workshop, Worcestershire
22–26 March	The Bike Shed Theatre, Devon
30 March	Small World Theatre, Ceredigion
1 April	Bleasdale Parish Hall, Lancashire
2 April	The Bureau, Lancashire
6 April	Riverside Theatre, Coleraine
7 April	Strule Arts Centre, Omagh
8 April	Waterside Theatre, Derry/Londonderry
9 April	The MAC, Belfast
13–30 April	The Salberg, Salisbury Playhouse, Wiltshire
3–4 May	The Stahl Theatre, Peterborough
6 May	Pentabus, Shropshire

This final performance will be streamed online and into Battersea Arts Centre.

Cast

BEA Rosie Armstrong

Rosie trained at Rose Bruford.

Theatre includes: *Dangerous Corner* (Theatre Royal Windsor and tour); *A Small Family Business* (National Theatre); *Chimerica* (Harold Pinter Theatre); *The Woman in Black* (Fortune); *Potted Panto* (Vaudeville); *Midnight* (Peacock); *Blair's Children* (Cockpit); *Casablanca* (Future Cinema); *The Incredible Doctor Guttmann* (KSP); *Miracle on 34th Street* and *In the Bleak Midwinter* (Farnham Maltings); *Sleeping Beauty* (Dukes, Lancaster); *I Am a Superhero* (Old Vic New Voices, Theatre503 Award); and four seasons for the Rude Mechanical Theatre Company.

Radio includes: *The Papers of A.J. Wentworth*, *The Change* and *Ring Around the Bath*, all for BBC Radio 4.

Rosie has recently filmed *Jack and Dean of all Trades* and *Ghost Fighting Corporation* for Colour TV.

JOSEPH Harry Long

Harry is Co-Artistic Director of Shanty Theatre Company.

Theatre includes: *Private Lives*, *The Family Way*, *Enemy of the People* (Octagon Theatre, Bolton); *Holy Mackerel* (Eastern Angles); *Fatal Attraction* (Theatre Royal Haymarket); *Words* (Clwyd Theatr, Cymru); *Aisles Apart*, *The Story Giant*, *The Rime of the Ancient Mariner*, *Smugglers* (Shanty Theatre Company); *An Inspector Calls* (English Theatre, Frankfurt); *The Importance of Being Earnest* (Regents Park Open Air Theatre); *Treasure Island* (Quantum Theatre).

Television includes: *The Hunt for Tony Blair*, *Lark Rise to Candleford*, *Doc Martin*, *One Summer*.

Radio includes: *The Avengers*.

Creative Team

WRITER Siân Owen

Siân Owen was the winner of the Oxford Playhouse New Playwriting Competition 2010 with her play *Restoration*. She has written for Pentabus (*This Land*); Box of Tricks (*Word:Play 4* at the Arcola); Dirty Protest (*Milgi's Yurt*, Cardiff); PLAYlist (Theatre503 and Latitude) and The Story Project (New Diorama, Southwark Playhouse). She also took part in the National Theatre/ Ty Newydd Habit of Art Writing Project. Siân was a member of the Sherman Cymru Advanced Writers Group and has been part of the Royal Court Studio Invitation Writers Group. She is a graduate of the prestigious MA Writing

Performance programme at Goldsmiths. Her plays include *This Land, Restoration, The Turn, Between The Sheets, I'm Thinking I Was Wrong, Classic, Pieces* and *Bad Blood.*

DIRECTOR Jo Newman

Jo is Assistant Resident Director at Salisbury Playhouse as part of the Regional Theatre Young Director's Scheme. She is Co-Artistic Director of Tin Box Theatre Company and part of the team managing PILOT Nights, Birmingham.

Directing credits as Co-–artistic Director of Tin Box Theatre include: *Stop the Clocks* (site-specific performance at Newman Bros Coffin Works); *Not Known at This Address* (BAC, mac Birmingham, The Last Refuge, Robinson Theatre); *Pint Dreams* (commissioned by mac, Warwick Arts Centre, Birmingham Repertory Theatre, Stan's Café and Black Country Touring); *The Salvagers* (work in progress showings at Birmingham Repertory Theatre and New Diorama Theatre). With Tin Box, Jo was a theatre maker on the Birmingham Rep Foundry Programme and part of New Diorama Theatre Emerging Theatre Companies Scheme 2013.

Assistant Directing credits include: *The Magna Carta Plays* (Salisbury Playhouse); *Bike* (Salisbury Playhouse); *Fallen Angels* (Salisbury Playhouse); *Clause 39* (Co-director, Salisbury Playhouse); *Little Shop of Horrors* (Salisbury Playhouse, Mercury Theatre Colchester); and *The Palace of Wasted Dreams* (Women and Theatre at mac Birmingham).

Jo has previously been on the Board of Directors for Sampad South Asian Arts, has worked as an Administration and Projects Assistant with Birmingham Opera Company, a script reader at the Birmingham Repertory Theatre, Visiting Lecturer at University of Wolverhampton and Dramaturg with Jerrel Jackson Dance Company.

DESIGNER Jean Chan

Jean Chan studied at the Royal Welsh College of Music and Drama. Graduating in 2008 with a BA Hons degree in Theatre Design, she went on to work as a resident designer, part of the Royal Shakespeare Company's Trainee Design Programme 2008–9. In 2009 she won the Linbury Biennial Prize for Stage Design. In 2013 Jean was shortlisted for the Arts Foundation Award in the category 'Design for Performance'.

Designs include: for Pentabus: *For Once, The Husbands and Mayfair*; *Much Ado About Nothing* (Queen's Theatre, Hornchurch); *Ticking* (Trafalgar Studios, London); *The Witches, James and the Giant Peach* and *The BFG* (Dundee Rep); *Hedda Gabler* (Royal Lyceum, Edinburgh); *Cyrano De Bergerac* (Royal & Derngate and Northern Stage); *Mother Courage, Bordergames, Tonypandemonium* (National Theatre Wales); *Hope Light and Nowhere*

(Edinburgh Fringe); *The Hairy Ape*, *The Irish Giant*, *The Seagull* (Southwark Playhouse); *The Suit* (Young Vic Theatre); *Hamlet YPS* (Royal Shakespeare Company); *The Garbage King* (The Unicorn Theatre); *1984*, *Alice by Heart* (Lyric Hammersmith); *I Have a Dream* (Polka Theatre); *When the Waters Came* (Theatre Centre); *Why the Lion Danced* (Yellow Earth Theatre); *The Birthday of the Infanta* (Trestle Theatre); *The Roman Bath* (Arcola Theatre); *Caucasian Chalk Circle* (Royal Welsh College of Music and Drama).

Associate and Co-designs include: *The James Plays* (National Theatre Scotland and National Theatre, London); *Lionboy* (Complicite); *Five Guys Named Moe* (Edinburgh and Theatre Royal Stratford East); *Monsters* (Arcola Theatre/Strawberry Vale Productions).

LIGHTING DESIGNER James Mackenzie

James trained at Rose Bruford College.

Credits include: for Pentabus: *Milked*; *Mmm Hmm* (Verity Standen); *TEN* (Tavaziva Dance); *By the Light of the Fool Moon* (Hocket and Hoot); *Dark Wood Deep Snow* (Northern Stage); *Dreaming in Code* and *In the Dust* (2Faced Dance); *Jason and the Argonauts* (Courtyard Theatre); *Close Distance* (Parlor Dance); *Finding Joy* (Vamos Theatre); *Rock and Suitcase Story* (Dance East); *The Legend of Captain Crow's Teeth* (Unicorn Theatre); *DNA* (Hull Truck); *Macbeth* (Courtyard Theatre); *Herding Cats* (Hampstead); *See* (Company Decalage); *Shattered* (Feral Productions); *Steam* (Royal Festival Hall); *Cut it Out* (Young Vic). James is also the Artistic Director of the award-winning ZOO Venues at the Edinburgh Festival Fringe.

SOUND DESIGNER James Frewer

James has a Master's degree in Conducting and Composition (University of Hull). He is an Associate Artist of Hull Truck.

Sound design credits include: for Pentabus: *Red Sky at Night*; *A Further Education* and *Deluge* (Hampstead Theatre); *Love Me Do* (Watford Palace Theatre); *The Ugly Sisters* (Rash Dash/National Tour).

Composition and music credits include: *Folk* (Birmingham Rep/Watford Palace/Hull Truck); *Get Carter* (Northern Stage); *Sleeping Beauty*, *Cinderella* and *A Taste of Honey* (Hull Truck); *Mercury Fur*, *Weekend Rockstars: An Album Play* (with Hull Truck); *Modern Life Is Rubbish: A Musical Manifesto* and *Saturday Night, Sunday Morning* (Middle Child Theatre); *The Thing About Psychopaths* (Red Ladder Theatre/National Tour).

Musical Director and performer credits include: *Dancehall* (Cast Doncaster); *The Night Before Christmas* (Soho Theatre); *This House* (National Theatre, dep performer).

SALISBURY PLAYHOUSE

Salisbury Playhouse is an arts and educational charity and one of Britain's leading producing theatres, with a national reputation for home-grown work of the highest quality that attracts audiences from across Wiltshire, Hampshire, Dorset and beyond.

The building comprises the 517-seat Main House, the 149-seat Salberg, a purpose-built Rehearsal Room and Community and Education Space. There is also an on-site scenery workshop, wardrobe and props store.

In addition to producing its own productions and welcoming the UK's leading touring companies, Salisbury Playhouse's extensive Take Part programme engages with more than 14,000 people of all ages each year, offering a range of creative learning, community and youth theatre activities.

As well as this production of *This Land*, Spring 2016 includes major revivals of *Hedda Gabler* and *Singin' in the Rain* (produced with the New Vic Theatre, Newcastle-under-Lyme, and Octagon Theatre, Bolton), the premiere of *Up Down Man* (produced with Myrtle Theatre Company) and the fifth Theatre Fest West, celebrating theatremakers from across the region.

Artistic Director	**Gareth Machin**
Executive Director	**Sebastian Warrack**

www.salisburyplayhouse.com

PENTABUS
RURAL THEATRE COMPANY

We are the nation's rural theatre company. We tour new plays to village halls and theatres, telling stories with local relevance and national impact.

Over four decades we've produced 150 new plays, supported 100 playwrights and reached over half a million audience members. We've won awards, pioneered live-streaming and developed a ground-breaking initiative to nurture young writers from rural backgrounds.

Over the next four decades we'll tour further than ever before, work with new and established playwrights, extend our young writers programme and continue to push at the boundaries of what theatre can be.

Pentabus is a registered charity (number 287909). We rely on the generosity of our donors, large and small, to help us to make brilliant new theatre.

You can find out more about us at **www.pentabus.co.uk**

Twitter **@pentabustheatre** | Facebook **Pentabus Theatre**

Pentabus Theatre Company, Bromfield, Ludlow, Shropshire, SY8 2JU

Pentabus is also supported by
The Millichope Foundation

Acknowledgements

My massive thanks to the following for their help and support on *This Land*:

Gareth Machin and all at Salisbury Playhouse.

To all at Pentabus. Elizabeth Freestone for her always wise words, calming influence, faith and belief in me. And to the team behind *This Land* and their amazing talents: James Frewer, James Mackenzie, Jean Chan, Jenny Pearce, Sam Eccles. And Jo Newman, thanks for coming with me on this epic journey, and for your belief and encouragement every step of the way.

Thank you to Ben Addis, Manjeet Mann, Charlotte Willis and Marc Willis for their help in the development of this piece.

Thanks also to John O'Donovan and all at Methuen Drama and Nick Quinn at The Agency.

And my endless gratitude to all my family and friends.

To Mum and Dad and Jonathan for their unwavering support and constant love.

For sticking by me through it all:

Alex Ferris, Amy and Chris Merrett, Craig Haywood, Chris Dainton, Gary Raymond, Kirsty and Mike Pattrick, Laura Wojtanowski, Lowri Culley, Lucy Mackenzie, Rhiannon Irigoyen, Rosie Goddard.

And to Daniel, Z and E. Thank you will never be enough. You are my superheroes.

This Land

for my grandparents

We do not inherit from our ancestors.
We borrow from our children.
Unknown

The Earth wasn't born with oil in it.
Rebecca Walsh Dell

Characters

all of whom should be played by the same two actors

Bea, *thirties*
Joseph, *thirties*
X
XX
Roman PR Consultant
Farmer
Birley
Aldrich
Applewood
Bund
Martha
Stanley
The Geologist
The Big Cheese
The Fairy Queen
An Archaeologist
A Volunteer

The play is set now and then.

Music marks the passing/shifting of time.

A solidus (/) indicates an interrupted line.

An ellipsis (. . .) indicates a hesitation or inability to find the right word.

Act One

Prologue

The first night home as three.

Fairy lights illuminate **Bea** *and* **Joseph**. **Bea** *is holding a tiny baby.*

Bea   This is our place.

This is your window.

This is your garden.

And those are the fields.

The patchwork quilt of fields that wrap around us here.

This is us.

Those lights are our neighbours.

Those lights are stars.

I'll tell you about stars another day.

Joseph   Maybe I should do that.

Bea   Yes. Good idea.

But first I am going to tell you about that field.

Joseph   The field you look at every time you look out of here.

Over there.

Bea   Because strange tales have been told about that field. It has seen dinosaurs roam and heard dragons roar.

Joseph   Um.

Bea   It has sat still as time has ticked and tocked and the ground has soaked it all up. It has stayed as things have come and gone and grown and died and flown over and fallen down. It has battled the elements and been burrowed into and it has secrets and stories buried deep inside.

Joseph   This isn't the version I remember.

Bea   It's a new version. Our new version.

Joseph   Right. But aren't you worried about filling his head with /

Bea   He is two days old.

Joseph   Exactly. There is so much to tell him. How everything works and what everything is and where do we even start?

Bea   Where did it start for us?

There is a tree in the corner of the field.

Joseph   Now this is the version I remember.

Bea   And once ago when the world wasn't as it is now, a lightning bolt hit it. Right in the heartwood.

Joseph   And the lightning spread through the branches and down into the roots and into the ground that lay beneath.

Bea   And the strike made scorch marks like splinters over all of the ground and made it look like the Earth was splitting apart. And tiny sparks burned on the end of each twig. Like so many fairy lights. And as they burnt they fell to the Earth.

And the ground smouldered.

Joseph   But there weren't fairy lights then.

Bea   Which is why some people say it was just fire.

Joseph   Because bulbs hadn't been invented.

Bea   But there are others that say it was actual fairies. Because people thought there were fairies living inside this patch of land. And they thought it was them. Making their own light. Trying to fix things. Forced out from where they were hidden by the crack and the shudder.

Joseph   Light bulbs, I mean. Not growing bulbs. Light bulbs hadn't been invented then. Growing bulbs had. Of course.

And candles.

And probably oil lamps.

Bea   And whatever you believe, regardless of what had and hadn't been invented then, the tree lit up.

And it was beautiful.

So beautiful, in fact, that the farmer who owned the field and the tree /

Joseph   I'm not sure he actually owned the /

Bea   The farmer stood and watched. Agog.

Joseph   A what?

Bea   Amazed. In awe.

Like we are now.

Like we are stood watching now.

Joseph   You are rocking.

Bea   You're rocking too.

Joseph   Oh yeah.

Bea   Like we are watching while rocking you now.

Joseph   I don't think the farmer was rocking though.

Bea   No. He was watching in wonder as the tips of the twigs burned and the earth smoked and then all the leaves fell off. All at once.

The lights flicker and go out.

Joseph   Are you sure?

Bea   And the ground slowly soaked up these scorched leaves and the soil swallowed them up. But the marks on the ground refused to go. And the farmer became very sad as he was certain that nothing could survive a strike like that.

But he couldn't bear to cut it down after what he had seen.

So the tree stayed there, lifeless. And nothing grew in the earth around it. Or so he thought.

Because as the next spring approached shoots started to appear in the earth there. Only they weren't green. They were orange.

Joseph   Brilliant flame orange. And they grew up from the ground and covered the field. It looked like the field itself was full of fire. And nobody could explain it.

Or, how, every now and again, over time, the earth would smoulder.

And strange smells would arrive on the wind.

Bea   So it seemed that there was some kind of magic in this field.

Something underneath.

Some said there was a dragon that had been woken by the lightning.

Some said there was treasure down there too.

Buried way back ago before even then.

Joseph   So as men have always done.

Bea   And women.

Joseph   They began to dig. Searching for what was beneath.

Scene One

An Iron Age settlement. 800 BC-ish. Dusk.

On their hands and knees is **XX**. *They are putting a sword into a hole in the ground.*

XX   I Chief Double X, offer these, swords of bronzest bronze, to give all the thanks for this happy harvest of finest foodage and fruitage and croppage.

You have given to us so I give to you.

This gift-age.

Of very best.

XX *draws a circle in the mud around the sword and covers it.*

X *comes racing on.*

X   Chief. There's been another one.

XX   Sshhh. I'm right in the middle of /

X   A clink. And it was really loud.

XX   You said the last one was a clank.

X   I did. But this one was more of a clink.

XX   Was it a clink or a clank?

X   I heard a clang.

It may have even been a clash.

And that's not all we've been hearing either, Chief.

There's stories from some of the other settlements too.

The word is . . .

XX   What?

X   Well, the word is, it's, it's, it is /

XX   WHAT IS THE WORD?

X   I-ron.

I-orn.

I-horn.

Metal.

There's some out there with a new kind of sharp.

A clanking clan.

And they might probably be coming for us.

So I think we should ready ourselves.

Where are our swords?

XX   In there.

X   What do you mean, in there?

XX   I just buried them. I was just doing the thanks.

Today is the day of the thanks.

X   Dig them back up.

XX   You can't make an offering and then dig it all back up again. We have just had the best harvest in fifteen years.

I had to give our best back.

X   We could explain.

We could put it all back later.

XX   I drew the circle and everything.

X   Then we're going to have to make more.

XX   What would be the point?

X   Really sharp ones?

XX   There's no copper left.

X   We could go and get some.

XX   It's too many darks and lights and walks away.

X   I've got a bronze bowl.

XX   That's not going to cut it.

X   So what are we going to do?

What are we going to use?

How are we supposed to get our fierce on if it's all in there?

XX   It isn't all in there.

Go and gather everyone.

X   But they are coming here with their clatter and we don't have anything to fight with.

XX   We have all of this to fight with.

We know this place.

We owe this place.

We were made here.

We have made here.

They don't know our nature.

So they can come here with all the iron they want . . .

XX *spits into the ground.*

X   Oh is *that* the word? It'll never catch on.

XX   But they haven't got our mettle, have they?

X   No. They have not.

XX   And they won't get this place.

X   They'll be coming here all – (*Marches.*)

And we'll be here all – (*Fierce.*)

We'll throw everything we've got at them.

XX   Yes. YES. Because we've. Got. Stones.

Loads of stones.

X   We do, don't we?

They begin to look for stones.

X   Giant ones.

XX   Yes we do.

X   And really really tiny ones.

XX   And middle-size ones.

And our stones can make axes.

X Yes, they can.

XX   And spears.

X   And really big circles.

XX   Hallelujah.

X   And we have wood.

XX   And grass.

X   And mud.

XX   So they can come here with all the clank they want. But this is ours.

And we need to show them what we are made of.

XX *rubs stones together to make a fire. It bursts into flames.*

X   Magic.

They do a war dance.

Scene Two

The pre-drilling preparatory stage.

The summer holidays. The countryside sings.

Two years have passed since we have last seen **Bea** *and* **Joseph**.

They are now in the field under the tree. **Joseph** *is covered in mud. He is covering* **Bea**'s *eyes and walking her towards a picnic all laid out on the ground.*

Joseph   Ta-dah!

He beams.

Bea   Oh no.

She looks around and buries her head in her hands.

Joseph   Not entirely the response I was hoping for.

Bea   We have a day on our own. A whole day.

A day of no potties or dinosaurs or tantrums.

Joseph   I'm not so sure about that.

Bea   We could have beer or be in a spa or a hotel or we could be asleep. Oh God, sleep. We could be in a whole bed that someone else will make. But instead you have walked me down the road into the field we look at every day.

Joseph   You weren't supposed to know where we were.

Exactly.

Bea   It sounds exactly like our garden.

We may as well be *in* our garden.

On our one day away, together, alone, in over two years, you have brought me five hundred metres from our house.

Joseph   Actually it is four hundred and twenty-three.

Bea   I can still see into our house, Joe. I can still see my mum and Dylan. He's climbing up on to the /

Joseph   Look over here. Here. To me. LOOK AT ME. Hello.

Bea   Hello.

Joseph   Hello.

Bea (*softening*)   Hello.

I put make up on and everything.

Joseph   You. Look. Beautiful.

Bea   I look pissed off.

Joseph   A bit.

This wasn't supposed to be shit.

Bea   I know.

Joseph   It is though, isn't it?

Bea   A bit.

Joseph   It's just there used to be magic in this field. Things used to happen in this field.

Bea   It's just a story.

Joseph   That wasn't what I was talking about.

We happened in this field.

Bea   Yeah. We did.

Joseph   Didn't we?

Bea   Yeah.

Joseph   And it's the summer holidays again.
And that's when we met.

1996.

I'd just arrived here.

You were always here.

And this is where we were.

This is what we did.

And this is where we'd run to.

This is where I could always find you.

Bea   We used to sneak out of school and run here.

Joseph   You'd run. I'd catch you up later.

Bea   You always were a bit slow on the uptake.

And a geek.

Joseph   I ran out of Geography with you once.

Bea   That's why you're a science teacher.

Joseph   We came and hid here.

Bea   And I don't know why, because my house is there.

Joseph   Everyone always came here.

Bea   Skiving. Smoking. Sheltering.

No wonder people think the earth smoulders.

All of us lighting up.

Joseph   But that day it was just us.

Bea   We'd just started going out.

Finally.

Joseph   Geography was the first lesson of the year.

And we ran for it.

Bea   Just to make that summer last a bit longer.

Joseph   Yeah.

And eventually it was always just us here.

Only us.

And I thought that would be good.

I thought we could hide again.

Bea   But we could have hidden anywhere.

Somewhere with a pool. Or a bar.

We could have hidden in a really expensive restaurant.

Joseph   I didn't want to go anywhere else.

Bea   You didn't fancy somewhere with chairs?

Joseph   Aha. HA.

He gets out a folding chair.

Joseph   It even has a space for a cup in the arm.

Bea   OK. Now I'm impressed.

Pause.

Joseph   I wanted us to go somewhere where we know where we are. I didn't want to go somewhere else. And then spend the whole time sorting and planning and looking at new stuff. I just wanted it to be us. I wanted us to know where we are because we haven't really had chance in a while, have we? And I thought it might be nice if we could just see where we are.

Bea   Well, here we are.

Joseph   Yeah.

Bea   I know. It's lovely.

Joseph   It's not, is it?

Bea   You're lovely for trying.

Joseph   I just wanted us back on a level playing field, Bea. You know?

Only it's not level, is it?

There's a massive hole in the ground over there, which I fell into.

Look at me.

Look at my best shirt.

What a mess.

Can we sort it?

Bea   We can try.

Joseph   There was never a hole there before.

She notices something and starts wandering off. She kicks a stake and uncovers some rope attached to it. It looks like something was or will be plotted out on the land.

Bea   This isn't usually here either.

She is distracted by what she has found.

Joseph   Bea. Can you come back?

Bea *is still looking at the ground.*

Joseph   Bea.

BEA.

She comes back towards him. He tries to be affectionate, hold her hand, hold her, but it is awkward.

Joseph   I don't know why I was thinking it would all be the same. We haven't been back here for so long.

Bea   I bring Dylan here all the time.

Joseph   Do you? Do you? You never said.

Bea   You never ask.

He loves to come and run around the field in the story.

And we look for dinosaurs and dragons and /

Joseph   Yeah. I was wondering, that story has got a bit − I mean, that wasn't exactly the story we were told . . . It's got a bit epic, hasn't it?

Bea   If you don't like it you can always do bedtime.

Joseph   No. Bea. That's not what I was . . . You know I can't. I can't get back in time.

Bea   It's the holidays.

Joseph   I know.

Bea   And you haven't done a bedtime since he was like in our arms tiny and now he's in his own bed big. He's two, Joe. That means I've done, like, seven hundred bedtimes.

Joseph   OK. OK. I could tonight?

Bea   Good.

Joseph   Good.

Pause.

But the thing is /

Bea   How did I know there would be a thing.

Joseph   I'm not as good as you at making stuff up.

That's not what I . . . I mean, you two have this whole . . . you two together . . . there is this . . . I don't know what . . . and I'm . . . I . . . I just don't know where you both are with everything.

I don't even seem to know where to start.

Bea   You could read him the telephone directory and he'd be happy.

Joseph   I'm a bit lost.

Bea   We are here. We are always here. We haven't gone anywhere.

I'm still here. Where you'd always find me.

Waiting for you.

If you looked.

Joseph   I do look.

Bea   I haven't seen you.

Joseph   You weren't looking at me to know.

Pause.

I don't want to go anywhere else.

Bea   Neither do I.

Joseph   So let's make a pact.

Let's come back here more often.

Let's make this a regular thing.

Bea   Once a week or something?

Joseph   Once a month?

We'll come down here.

With food.

Bea   And wine.

Joseph   In a cup.

Bea   Just me and you.

Date nights.

Joseph   I was thinking afternoons.

Bea   You're going to pull sickies?

Joseph   I was thinking weekends.

Bea   Oh right.

Joseph   To start with. We need to start somewhere.

And anywhere is better than where we are now.

Bea   OK.

Joseph   OK?

Bea   Yeah.

Joseph   YEAH.

I know it's not all that exciting.

But this is our place.

It's special.

I'll make it special.

We'll find a day every month.

I promise.

I promise to find a day every month.

Here. Where it can just be us.

I promise that.

I promise to not let anything else stop it being just us.

Bea   Those aren't our footprints.

Scene Three

Dylan's bedroom later that day.

Bedtime.

Joseph *is sitting with a pile of books.*

Joseph   So the thing is, little man, I'm not so good at stories.

Not like your Mummy does.

Not The Story.

I know. I'm sorry.

But look. I thought I'd bring in some of the books that Daddy reads every day.

These are all the ones I carry in my work bag.

And I thought you might like to choose.

There are books on

Atoms, elements and the periodic table.

Space.

Plants.

Fossil fuels.

What do you fancy? You can choose.

No, Dylan. That's post. That I didn't open yet.

You want what's in there?

OK. OK. OK. It looks like it even might have pictures.

'The Search for Unconventional Gas' /

Aha! This sounds like our kind of thing.

'Has come to your area.' Oh.

He reads.

'Dear Resident,

'This is a letter to update you that planning permission has been granted allowing us to undertake testing for shale gas at the site highlighted in blue on the map below.'

Pause.

What is hydraulic fracturing?

Hydraulic fracturing is the process of drilling down deep into the Earth and injecting a special liquid, a mixture of water, chemicals and proppants, at high pressure to fracture the shale rock which allows gas, otherwise trapped, to be extracted and brought back up to the surface.

There are differing stages to the process.

1) Preparing the site and constructing the well pad.

2) Drilling.

3) Hydraulic fracturing.

4) Flow testing.

Each stage is fully explained in the leaflet included.

We understand the need you may have for more information so we have organised a community engagement day.

This is our chance to explain the phases of work that will be undertaken.

This is your chance to ask us questions.

Enclosed is more information on the key topics that can be discussed further on the day:

Seismic.

Traffic.

Noise.

Light.

Water.

Bea.

Bea.

BEA.

Scene Four

AD 193. Morning. Complete quiet apart from birds singing.

A **Roman** *PR consultant, in armour, approaches a* **Farmer** *who is harvesting their crops.*

Roman   SALVE! Quid agis?

Farmer   How do.

Roman   May I just ask what it is you do do?

Farmer   I am digging. Diggio. Spade. Spadeis. Spade. Is.

Roman   Shouldn't you be starting over there?

Farmer   Why?

Roman   The plans clearly state /

Farmer   What plans?

Roman   Right. Can I just double check. Who are you?

Farmer   I'm whose field you're standing in, mate.

Roman   I see. Did you not get the edictum?

Farmer   Actually could you just stand a bit back. A bit more. A bit more. All the way. That's it. Watch out for the /

Roman   Sorry. Sorry.

Farmer   CAREFUL.

Roman   Excuse me . . .

Farmer   Just keep still.

Roman   I just wanted to check if you had seen. There was a sign.

Farmer   Did you see it too? I have never seen birds fly like that before.

It's why I'm getting it all out now. It's a bit early, but /

Roman   A sign about the permission.

Farmer   I don't need permission to dig my own land, mate.

Roman   Permissu aedificare via.

Farmer   Now you've lost me.

Roman   No, follow me, it should be here somewhere.

Farmer   Hey. Hey. HEY. Stop. You're trampling all over the /

Roman   Somewhere . . .

Farmer   You lot coming here in your suits.

Roman   Juuussssst . . .

Farmer   Turnips.

Roman   HERE.

Farmer   WATCH OUT FOR THE TURNIPS.

The **Roman** *moves greenery to uncover an engraved stone obelisk.*

Roman   AHA!

Farmer   What is this?

Roman   Animadvertitie.

Nothing.

Notice. A notice for you.

Farmer   For me personally?

Roman   For you and your neighbours.

Farmer   What is it doing there?

Roman   It's there for you to see.

Farmer   But I am over here.

Roman   Yes, but when you go past here.

Farmer   I never go down there.

Roman   But here it is.

Farmer   And I am here. I am busy being over here. Now if you don't mind I've got to get all this up.

Roman   So you haven't seen it?

Farmer   I have never seen that before.

Roman   You can see it now though.

Farmer   Yes. There it is.

Roman   Come. And. See.

Farmer   Why don't you read it out for me?

Roman   It's just the usual . . .

'Application RRAD193. The above order made by the Roman Empire. Notice hereby given blah blah blah of construction and maintenance of a highway, da de da, two chariots' span, et cetera et cetera, carrying out of works on watercourses in conjunction with aforesaid construction, drainage facilities incorporated, provision of new means of access to planned premises, dum de dum, improving surroundings thereof. Any objections need to be made in writing to Town Planning, Britannia Department, Senate House, Rome. Before 13th October of this year.'

And that was yesterday.

Farmer   You lot do like your words.

Roman   Actually those are your words.

Farmer   I knew that. I knew that. I have just never heard them before in that particular order.

Roman   I see.

Farmer   Right you are then. Thanks for letting me know.

Carries on digging.

Farmer   All that was on there?

Roman   It is quite a tome. And very small writing.

Farmer   So what you are telling me /

Roman   Not me, exactly, I am merely making sure /

Farmer   So what you're telling me is that there's going to be a road?

Roman   Yes.

Farmer   Where exactly?

Roman   It'll be right about . . . here.

The **Roman** *stands exactly where the* **Farmer** *is digging.*

Farmer   I see.

Roman   Oh, good.

Farmer   And what if I did happen to object now?

Roman   Well, I'm afraid that's too late. You see, I am here with a *decretum admoveo*.

Farmer   Then you'd better get going and sort that out.

Roman   No. You don't understand.

Farmer   I do. Move it.

Roman   I can't.

Farmer   Out of my way.

Roman   Plebian. You are impedirent.

Farmer (*incensed*)   I'm what?

Roman   In. The. Way.

Pause.

Look. The plans are very clear. We gave you plenty of warning. Twenty-one whole days. It was all there. In stone.

All we ask is that you move. Slightly.

Farmer   How slightly?

Roman   I'm so sorry I don't have the exact plans on me now. I couldn't carry them all with me. But I would hazard a guess of . . . ooo, the next town.

Farmer   That is a day away.

Roman   Perfect.

We appreciate your inconvenience so perhaps we can help you?

Farmer   I don't want your help.

Roman   Compensation. Damages.

Farmer   I'll damage you in a minute.

Roman   You can't stand in the way of progress.

The **Farmer** *stands in the* **Roman**'*s way.*

Roman   It's coming straight for you.

Watch.

The **Roman** *knocks the* **Farmer** *out of the way as the* **Roman** *marches the route, arms waving, demonstrating where the road is going, walking all over the unharvested crops.*

Roman   Via a go-go, via a go-go, via a go-go.

Farmer   No no no no no. No.

The **Farmer** *grabs the* **Roman**'*s cloak and in doing so pulls off a brooch, throws it into the ground and stamps on it.*

Roman   AH. MY BROOCH.

Pause. The **Roman** *retains composure.*

Roman   Protest noted. But, you see, the thing is, that if you don't go there will be, um, how best to say this, I can't think of how to put this exactly . . .

Farmer   Oh come on. You're the one with all the words.

Roman   Yes. Yes. I do have one.

Farmer   And what is that?

Roman   Mortifero.

Farmer   Oh.

Beat.

About those damages?

Scene Five

Preparing the site / constructing the well pad.

The field is fenced off for construction of the drill pad. **Bea** *and* **Joseph** *are standing behind the metal fence that is now surrounding the field. They can't get in.* **Joseph** *is carrying a picnic basket.*

Joseph   This wasn't here this morning.

I thought we had more time before they built the well pad.

Bea   Is it electric?

Joseph   No. It's gas. They're looking for gas.

Bea   I. Was. Talking. About. The. Fence.

Joseph   Oh. Ha. Sorry. NO. No. Why would it be? Would it be? I don't know. I don't think so. I'll check.

Bea   How do we check?

Joseph *throws his shoe at it.*

Joseph   No. Ha. No.

He tentatively taps it.

They both put their heads up against the fence.

Bea   I think this is the end of our summer.

Joseph   No way. We can get over this.

Bea   We can't. Can we?

Joseph   There's nobody in there.

Come on.

It's not like we haven't done this before.

Bea   We have never done this before.

Joseph   Then it's time we tried.

He tries to lift **Bea** *over but they just can't work it out.*

Bea   Joseph. I think we have reached our autumn.

Joseph   No. No. Hang on. Why? Why is it our autumn? I don't like that idea at all.

Bea *sits down, defeated. She starts to unpack the picnic.*

Bea   This is awful.

Can we eat? I can't wait any more. I've had half a fish finger today.

Joseph   OK. OK. But autumn is nice. There's leaves. And walks. And it isn't winter, is it?

And actually winter is great. Winter is my favourite. Apart from the summer. And the autumn. Winter is all romantic with the twinkly lights and mistletoe and scarves and fire. Cuddling up in front of the fire. And then, and then comes spring again.

Bea *doesn't say anything.*

Joseph *is determined to get them over the fence and looks for ways to do it.*

Joseph   And autumn now isn't like when we were kids. I mean, it was all so clear cut then. Everybody knew where they were. It was all in order. It was wellies and vests and stamping on leaves then it was cold on the end of your nose winter with snow days and gloves with the string that gave you robot arms and then too hot for hats spring and then going down hills on your bikes to catch a breeze summers. Now we just don't know where we are. It's not straightforward any more. One day it is autumn in the morning then it could be spring in the afternoon. So if it does feel like autumn right now it isn't as bad as you think.

Although you are a bit right.

This is awful.

I should have just booked us a restaurant. But I made you a promise. And I wanted to keep it.

And we already had to miss our last date because of that information day thing.

Pause.

And I didn't want to not keep it again.

But it looks like I can't. Not here anyway.

Bea   Where do we go now?

Joseph   We need to find somewhere else. A new place.

(*Thinking*) But you were also totally right about it almost being our garden.

Let's just go to our garden.

Bea (*unimpressed*)   Brilliant.

Joseph   That can be our new place.

Bea   It already is our place. And it's a shit tip.

Joseph   I'll do it up. Make it proper. We can meet there instead. Same deal. Same promise. I'll get a table and some chairs. And one of those heaters.

Bea   It did use to be so lovely. When I was a kid.

Joseph   I will make it lovely. Or or we could do it all together?

We could even dig a patch in the garden together.

Plant some seeds.

Bea   Yes. There used to be loads of stuff growing when Gran lived here.

Joseph   That's what we'll do. Get Dylan to help

And get him a slide. And a swing and a /

Bea   How am I going to tell him that we can't come here any more?

What am I going to say?

We even left his wooden sword over there.

Joseph   We can have a think about what to say now if you like?

Bea   Yes. Please.

*A timer alarm goes on **Joseph***'s phone.*

Bea   Oh.

Joseph   I'm sorry. It's just I have that lesson plan for Year 9 to write.

For the inspection.

And then there's that big village meeting tonight.

Bea   It's bedtime soon anyway.

I guess I'll do the story?

Joseph   We just need to hang on. Wait it out.

This might be autumn but I won't let us fall apart.

I will make a new place for us and I will meet you there on our date. We can turn it all back around again. I mean, there has never been a time when there wasn't a spring or summer again.

Pause.

Apart from the Dark Ages.

Scene Six

1348.

Daytime, but there is an unearthly light.

Two buriers of the dead, **Birley** *and* **Aldrich***, are pushing a cart laden with bodies of those who have died from the plague. A bell hangs from the cart. It rings as they move. It is raining hard. And windy. It is hard work. They have flower posies around their necks. Around* **Birley***'s neck is also a bottle of vinegar and some willow.*

Birley   WIND.

They cover their faces with flowers that hang around their necks.

The bell on the cart rings louder in the wind.

Aldrich   That blasten bell.

You must be used to it.

Do you get used it it?

You must have.

Birley *doesn't respond.*

Aldrich   They said that if I was to do this then you were the man to do it with.

Birley Bones.

You *know*. You are still here. You know how to still be here.

And I can see you've got lots of things all round your neck. You are carrying a lot of neckynges there.

Do I need all that then? Because nobody said anything about that. They just told me to meet you and that you'd tell me what to do and /

Birley   WIND.

They cover their faces again.

Aldrich   Because they never told me about any neckynge.

Nothing.

They say that you've lasted longer than anyone. And I know
it's only my first day and I don't mean to be asky or anything
but you haven't said more than two words, one of them being
WIND, all the day and I just think if we are going to be
walking together and toiling then maysbe you could give me
a few pointers, show me the way?

Birley   Where did they find you?

Aldrich   Prison.

Birley   WIND.

Aldrich   Do you really have to do that all the day? I do pick
things up very quickly.

Birley   I'm sure you will.

Aldrich   And I really don't want to talk out of turn, but I
think we might be going the wrong direction? I wonder that
maysbe the pit we need is over there. That way is to town you
see /

Birley   Stop. Right. There.

Birley *stops pushing the cart and takes out a spade for each of them and
throws it at* **Aldrich***, who catches it.*

Aldrich   What you doing?

Birley   Stopping here.

Birley *takes all neckynges off.* **Aldrich** *goes over to the pile of stuff to
have a look.*

Birley   Don't touch that.

Aldrich *goes towards the cart.*

Birley   Don't touch any of them ones either.

Aldrich   I just want to see what it looks like up close. Those
boils are pretty nastye, aren't they?

Birley   You wanted my advice didn't you?

Aldrich   You can't get it by touching them. And I've got my flowers on.

Birley   Dig.

Aldrich   You can't do this here.

Birley   Dig.

Aldrich   It's not a *special* place.

Birley   Yes. It. Is. Look at it. It's beautifous.

Aldrich   I mean /

Birley   I know what you mean.

Aldrich   But all this has growings and crops and plants and The Green?

Birley   Exactly.

Aldrich   Whose field is this?

Birley   It doesn't matter.

Aldrich   Yes, it does.

Birley   Look at it. All oversprung. There's been no harvest here. It's wild. So if they're not already gone they will be soon.

Aldrich   But there are rules.

Birley   And thems what wrote them /

Aldrich   The men of clever?

Birley   Yes. They're all six feet under.

Aldrich   Exactly. They told me there are measurements how far down they need to be put and and we don't have any of the /

Birley   I know what I am doing.

Aldrich   Shamefaste.

Birley   Don't you want to end up somewhere decent?

Birley *digs into the land.*

Aldrich   Stop. STOP IT.

Birley   You want to know how I have lasted so long?
Because I never go near any of those stinkynge pits. Them
that I pick up get put somewhere decent.

Everyone deserves a restful spot.

Birley *carries on digging.*

Aldrich   Stop. Please. Stop it. There are special places that
we are supposed to put them that have got the bad. Agreed
places. You know, by the clever. There are laws. And I would
have said twelve full moons ago that they can stick their laws
where the sun doesn't shine but I have seen things in the sky
that I shouldn't and it just keeps raining and then there's this
WIND. We need to get them in before it all spreads. But we
can't go putting them anywhere. That's wycked. We have to
do it all proper.

And here isn't right.

Birley   Here is just right. I'd like to be put here.

Aldrich   You can't be opening doors here. You can't put *that*
in there. The Yuckage and The Noxic and The Fume. You
can't put all them poisoned in there. You need to put it in
places where people know. You can't be just putting that in
anywhere. It needs markages so everybody knows not to go
near. Knows never to touch it again.

You shouldn't mess.

Don't go digging.

Birley   Either you help me put them in there, or you're
going in with them.

Scene Seven

The drill rig is being assembled.

Bea *is digging the vegetable patch in the garden.*

Joseph *is late. Again.*

Joseph   I am so sorry.

Bea   There. Are. So. Many. Stones.

Joseph   You must be freezing. Have my jacket.

Bea   No.

Joseph   You used to love wearing my jacket.

Bea   I used to love the smell of your aftershave.

Silence between them, but there is noise from the drilling site.

Joseph   Let me do some of that.

She won't let him.

Bea   Please?

She digs harder.

Joseph   I'm so sorry, Bea. I got caught up with something at work.

And there was a mountain of marking and the new timetables and /

Bea   It's Saturday.

Joseph   And then my laptop died. And there were loads of phone calls about this village meeting with that MP tonight, then as I was cycling home one of those lorries came past and I was miles away and I was just trying to get back to you and I just wasn't expecting it and I had to swerve and then I was in a ditch. And then I got a puncture. I'm sorry.

His phone rings. He doesn't answer it.

Bea   Why do you have to go tonight?

There's a 125-foot rig going up. There.

The drilling will start any day.

It is all in motion.

All spiralling out of control.

So what is the point?

Other than the one about to be drilled thousands of metres under our house.

Bea *sticks the spade in the ground.*

Joseph *takes it.*

Joseph   Are you sure you don't want to come?

You're so good at being angry.

Bea   Give me that spade.

Joseph *does. Silence as* **Bea** *carries on working on the patch.*

Bea   Carrots or parsnips?

Joseph   Oh.

Bea   Carrots or parsnips? To go in here. Now.

Joseph   Have you got the instructions?

It's just it might not quite be the time of year /

Bea   Can. You. Please. Just. Decide. Something.

Carrots or bastard parsnips?

Joseph   Carrots.

Bea   Sorry. There are just so many questions, you know in a day. I need to have so many answers. How do lights work, what are roads, what is that, why are you doing that, where are all those lorries going, how does a bird fly, what are they building, how high is it going to be, how high are planes, how does a plane fly, why are there clouds, how does rain, how does a bull doze, what is that down there, what is mud made of, where are my shoes, where is my wooden sword, where is Daddy?

Joseph   Sorry.

Bea   And I don't have all of the answers.

I think maybe it would better if we swapped.

Joseph   Good. Right. Let me.

He tries to take the spade off her.

Bea   Because I'm not sure that another day of him eating just rice cakes and fish fingers is totally /

Joseph   It's fine.

Bea   And you cook better.

Joseph   He is fine.

Bea   And you know everything.

Joseph   You are a natural.

Bea   I'm not. This isn't what I thought it was going to be, you know.

Joseph   I know.

Bea   Do you?

Joseph   Maybe not.

Bea   I thought I knew what being a mum would mean.

What I would be able to do. What I would be like.

I wanted to be all home-grown and fresh and bare feet and sunshine.

I try so hard.

I'm just not very good at it.

I can't even open an organic baby-food pouch. Why do they make those lids so, you know . . . unbreakable.

That's what I wanted to be.

Shouldn't it be in the genes? Mum used to make everything all like wholesome and Gran she was some war Land Girl goddess who dug victoriously. They struck gold. They could just do it. All. And it's the same earth, isn't it? All the fields round here. I think Gran even used our field to grow. Our garden. Everything they had, I have. It's the same bloody house. And I just can't seem to manage the same.

Joseph   You have other stuff going on.

Bea   So did she. You know. They had like an actual war. And she lost her husband. She had all that.

Joseph   You have a tiny human.

Bea   So did she. She was just pregnant with my mum when she lost him. And she carried on. She kept it all going.

Joseph   Look what you did today. You and Dylan did this today.

Bea   We managed ten minutes and then there was like stuff and noise and strange smells and building bangs and clanks and he didn't like it any more. I didn't like it any more.

Joseph   We could all try again tomorrow.

Bea   He *has* gone to sleep in his wellies.

Joseph   Has he? You see?

Bea   I couldn't actually get one of them off.

Joseph   Right.

Bea   And if he wasn't crying enough, we could only find one of his torches at bedtime.

Joseph   Torches?

Bea   He has two.

Joseph   Why.

Bea   Because he is two. And it just is.

Joseph   And I should know.

Bea   And then we looked out of the window.

They have cut down the fucking tree.

They have started building the rig.

And that's it, isn't it.

You should have seen it.

And I was hoping that we could get it back.

But now its changed.

We can't go back.

Look at it.

Joseph   No.

Bea   Look at it.

Joseph   I don't want to look at it.

I don't want to talk about it.

We agreed, we weren't going to talk about it, when it was just us.

I want to look at you.

She won't look at him.

Bea   I'm not sure I can do this. Christ, Joseph, you know it was hard enough anyway. Just. The world. Just getting out.

Getting on. Keeping him safe.

Just being in charge of this tiny thing. Only that's just it. When he was tiny I could just keep him here, in my arms. And I could feel him breathe and watch him and he was just here.

And you were here.

And now you are never are.

Even after you promised.

You are always running somewhere else.

And so is he.

Now he can run too.

He can run so fast.

And there's no stop button.

And so everything now is just. You know.

ARGH.

Who knew?

That everything could be so dangerous.

Batteries, plugs, walls, radiators, drawers, the kitchen, sharp things, edges, flat things, step things, kerbs, roads.

And that was before all of this.

All of this.

How do I explain all of this?

All of this arriving here?

I don't even understand all of this.

So much stuff.

Stuff that shouldn't be here.

We counted fifty lorries today.

And their wheels are like three of him and half of me and they have taken away where we went to be safe and just to run it all out and let off steam and now there is stuff in the air, I don't know what and dust and noise and grit and cranes and clank and monster drills and everything is massive and we are so small. He is so small.

And this was our place.

Where we were safe.

Where we were us.

Just us.

How do we keep him safe now?

Joseph   We can get over this.

I'm not going to let this /

Bea   I don't think there's anything you can do.

Joseph   I will do whatever it takes.

His phone rings. He throws it into the mud and stamps on it.

Bea   I'm not sure that's going to be enough.

Joseph   I'm not sure you even want to work it out.

Bea   I'm not sure I want to be here any more.

Joseph   I'm not sure you love me any more.

She doesn't move.

Joseph   Beatrice.

Bea.

A low rumble.

Bea   I do.

But I think there's a leak.

The Earth under him crumbles slightly.

I think I have sprung a leak and it's escaping.

Just a little bit.

Every day.

Every day you miss something else.

Every day we aren't first.

Every day we lose a bit more.

And I don't know how to stop it.

And I don't know where it's all going.

The rumbles get louder and louder.

Scene Eight

1770. A field of furrows.

Applewood *is pushing on a crate. It is really heavy.* **Bund** *stands arms folded.*

Bund   Look what the wind's blown in.

Applewood   Have you seen those clouds?

They've followed me back.

I thought it was just the smoke at first.

That steam smog.

So many chimney stacks have sprouted up there.

You can't even see the sky in parts.

But there is one mighty storm brewing.

Those clouds are full of lightning.

I thought I'd escaped it but no.

Looks like I've walked right into the face of thunder.

Bund   You only went to get a new rake.

Applewood   Yes, now /

Bund   Three days ago.

Applewood   You see what happened was /

Bund   Where's the rake?

Applewood   Now the thing is /

Bund   What is that?

Applewood (*putting a foot proudly on the box*)   *This* is the thing.

Bund   Is it?

Applewood   This is the future.

Bund   That's a box.

Applewood   This is just one of the boxes.

The others are on the cart.

Bund   What cart?

Applewood   The cart I had to get to carry all of this here.

Bund   You left me here to do all the scattering /

Applewood   Never again my dear /

Bund   The weather is breaking /

Applewood   will you ever /

Bund   My back is broken /

Applewood   – ever have to do that again /

Bund   And you come back here with, wait, what did you say?

Applewood   I was trying to tell you that, this, here is an end to all of that.

This here is the beginning of a life of quick.

A life of less hard work.

A life of more.

Bund   More boxes?

Applewood (*opening the box*)   This is the Jethro Tull Seed Drill.

Nothing.

Applewood   Obviously we need to put it all together.

Silence.

Obviously I need to put it all together.

But when I do this machine will change everything.

Bund   I have never heard of anything so ridiculous.

Applewood   There is an iron plough at the front /

Bund   A machine that drills on its own?

Applewood   – and the seeds will fall from the seed box /

Bund   How far will it all go?

Applewood   As far down as you want it to /

Bund   Next you'll be telling me it covers them up as well.

Applewood   And then the harrow at the back will cover the seeds so that none of them will get lost.

Bund   Oh.

Applewood   And it will do all of this in a straight line. Three. Rows. At. A. Time. Power. Planting.

Silence.

Applewood   The man at the shop explained it much better. He said they were flying out of the door.

Bund   Silly man. As if anything but birds will ever fly.

Bund *starts looking at the pieces in the box.*

Bund   What's this?

Applewood   That's the seed box.

Bund   Won't it make the food all a bit . . . sharp?

Rooting around the box.

What's this?

Applewood   That's the iron plough bit.

Bund   What's that?

Applewood   That's the rotating cylinder.

Now don't start mixing it all /

Bund   I'm not sure about the churn on that.

Applewood   Just leave the thing-a-me-bob /

Bund   And this?

Applewood   That's the thing-a-me-jig.

Bund   I think someone has led you a merry dance.

Applewood   You wait.

Just wait.

When I get this up and running.

This is a feat of engineering.

They're not going to be able to walk all over us any more.

Bund   How much did it cost?

Applewood   This is priceless.

Bund   We don't have anything spare.

Applewood   Imagine if we did.

Spare and more.

All the time.

For us to eat.

For us to sell.

Please stop touching everything.

There's an order.

Bund   What's wrong with using our hands?

Applewood   What's wrong with not?

Bund   That wind is picking up.

Applewood   Change is coming.

And it is coming full steam, straight for us.

Applewood *picks up the instructions. Turns them round the other way.*

Bund   It does all look very complicated.

Applewood   Exactly.

Bund   So it must be good.

Applewood   Progress.

Bund   Who am I to stand in the way of that?

Applewood   Once this is up and running you can stand all you like.

Bund   What is that bit?

Applewood   That's where the horse goes.

Bund   We don't have a horse.

Applewood   Ah now, so that was the other thing I needed to tell you about.

Thunder and lightning/rumbles.

Scene Nine

*A few hours on from when we last saw **Bea**. She is telling Dylan his bedtime story.*

Bea   And the thing is little man, is that we all have to learn to share. Even when we don't want to.

Things change.

Even when we don't want them to.

But that is the way of the world.

And our bit of the world has just got a bit stranger.

But that's OK.

Because what you have to remember and hold in your mind is that it is because that field is magic.

We live where trees fell and mammals and animals and mini-animals, and dinosaurs fell on top of them and more trees and debris and things that had reached their end and more on top of more on top of more and all that weight and time and stuff and things, in that particular order, well it was the perfect recipe.

We live in a special place, and when people began to dig here they found a certain kind of treasure.

Bits of it are buried all over the Earth, all under the Earth, and you can't see it but we have some here.

I know!

And that is what is going on over there.

They are digging for that treasure.

I KNOW! And when they find it, because it is buried so far down they have to try really hard to get it out. So there will be strange noises and smells and sounds and sights that you haven't seen before.

And it may wake up some of the other creatures from our story.

Sometimes you might see a dragon breathing out fire but he is a very friendly dragon, like the one in our game, and sometimes you might hear him humming or or or you might feel him walking and because he's so big things may shake a bit. And and and you might see the new tower, the new metal tower, the new knight's turret that he has built to make sure he can watch over the dragon.

The fairies might even come and see what all the racket is.

Or or or you might see trucks and diggers and lorries and cement-mixers and tractors and cranes and fuel tankers.

I know! Just like in your book.

And because they are looking for this treasure that is so hard to see they need to turn the lights on really bright, even at night, so we'll need to get you new special curtains.

Of course dinosaur ones.

And you may need to wear special things on your ears for a bit. Because looking for treasure is noisy.

And so it will all be a bit upside down and inside out for a while.

But one day we will get it back.

But not for a while.

And when we do it might not quite be as we had it before.

You know, when you lent one of your dinosaurs to your friend Max and it came back a bit different.

No. It won't be broken. But it might look different.

It was a bit of a different shape, wasn't it?

And while all this is going on we can't go into our field.

I know. I know.

Mummy is so sad too.

But they are just borrowing it.

And we have to be brave.

Really brave.

Noise, light, headlights, dragons' eyes, towers, rumbles.

The landscape changes.

Their world isn't the same any more.

End of Act One.

Act Two

Scene One

Joseph *is in his classroom. As he talks he does science experiments with light/fire/gas.*

Joseph In you come. In you come.

That's it. Coats off. Bums on seats.

Blackout.

Oh. Oh no. Oh, hang on.

Everyone stay still.

If you could all just stay where you are, please.

What has happened to the lights?

Just stay where you are everyone.

I need to find some light.

Everyone just hang on.

Put that lighter away, Joshua.

Aha. What I have got here?

He makes light – a candle, a Bunsen burner.

There you are Year 9.

And how lovely you all look. In the dark.

Now I know this won't come as a surprise to you bright sparks, but there haven't always been lights that just come on.

There hasn't always been power and electricity.

We have had to find that.

People have had to work it all out.

The light changes.

It has taken millions of years to make what we have got now.

And we know because if we look hard enough we can tell what has come before.

There are people who read the Earth like we read books.

And they can tell us stories of floods and fires and famines and fates.

Of battles and burials and births.

Because when you dig into the earth you are actually travelling through time and you can see how those that came before lived.

The Earth holding clues to all of it.

Metres of millennia.

And we can use all of this information that we find beneath us.

Some of what we find goes in museums.

Some of it goes in books.

Some of it goes into science.

Some of it goes to help us with all the things we need today. And today we are going to look at how we are travelling back millions of years to power our today. And have a think about what other options there may be. Because it isn't a bottomless pit.

Although some of it is very far down.

Thousands of metres down in the case of the shale gas they're extracting here.

So buried that they actually need to blast it out.

With millions of gallons of fracking fluid.

No, Joshua.

I said fracking.

We'll save that for Biology, shall we?

Right now we're talking Chemistry and Technology and History.

Right now they are pumping in millions of gallons of water and sand and chemicals to travel millions of years down to get gas to power our population of millions.

Because what if we lose all of this?

All of this light and warmth and fire and spark?

We are so used to it all being there.

Like it always has been.

We take it for granted.

But we need to start thinking about what happens if it isn't there any more.

Power cuts maybe just around the corner.

Apparently in 2013 Britain was six hours away from running out of gas. And it's not like it hasn't happened before.

In 1973 the Government introduced a three-day week and energy was rationed because of an energy crisis.

In the 1940s we had to keep the lights off for a very different reason. But it may be good to think about how everyone coped. At these times of darkness and crisis.

He pours liquid light into a glass.

We are so used to turning a switch on and light pouring in that it is hard to think about it all not being there when we need it.

But the situation is very precarious.

We have to try harder. Think more about what we're doing.

Because otherwise the world could be a very dark place.

Scene Two

1941.

An air-raid siren sounds, planes overhead.

Martha, **Bea**'s *grandmother, is lying in amongst the vegetable patches. She is working as a Land Girl.* **Stanley**, *the farm owner's son, comes to find her.*

Stanley   We've been looking for you everywhere.

Martha   I've been here.

Stanley (*helping her up*)   You don't have to be here today.

They sit on the side of the vegetable patch.

Martha   I have to be here.

Stanley   You only heard yesterday. You can have today, at least.

Martha   I'm not sure your father would agree.

Stanley   He's the one who wanted me to send you home.

Martha   I signed up to be here every day.

I'm not letting one of the other girls carry my load.

Stanley   Maybe they want to help carry yours.

Martha   I need to be here.

Stanley   Martha.

You don't look well.

Martha   I feel sick.

Stanley   You look so cold.

At least put a coat on.

You'll catch your death.

Martha   Good.

I'm hoping it's contagious.

Stanley   You could always come and help me with the /

Martha   I AM STAYING HERE.

He stood here. There.

He came to say goodbye. Before reporting back for duty.

'All this planting.

All this growing.

Look at all this good,' he said.

And he held my hand.

And squeezed it.

Pause.

I am mulch.

I think I may freeze.

Can blood freeze?

Can your heart?

Because that's what it felt like.

When they told me.

Even though all of us are expecting it.

There was always hope.

And now there is just the cold and all these cracks.

It feels like my Earth is splitting apart.

I don't know how I will ever put myself back together again.

Stanley   We've survived lightning strikes here before. This place fights back. You need to fight back.

Martha   I want him back.

I. Want. Him. Back.

Why can't they bring any of them back? At least then there would be part of him, somewhere I could sit by. Because he'd be here. He'd be in. But somewhere else has him. Them. And there will always be a whole layer missing.

I thought here would help.

But there's nothing of him.

Even his footprints have gone.

There's nowhere. There's nowhere for me to go.

There's nowhere for it to go.

All of this . . .

There are no words so she makes a noise as a bit of her breaks.

All of this without him.

All this time without him.

Stanley   Put it all in there.

He tries to give her a spade.

Put it all in there.

Dig deep.

Break apart.

Get it all out.

All the bad.

And then when you're ready, perhaps you'd like to plant some of these seeds.

These always seem to make it through the frost.

Even if that just gets you through the first minutes, the first hours, the first days.

At least you are doing something.

You feel like you're doing something.

Making something good out of all of this.

Dig for Victory.

Even if that just means getting through today.

Put everything into that.

Martha   But it's not everything, is it?

It still isn't enough.

There will always be something missing.

And I need something of him.

In there.

This place can't be without him.

I can't be without him in this place.

He so loved it here.

Stanley   He so loved you.

Martha   I need something of his.

Something to make a mark.

Something to leave.

We keep finding all these bits and pieces, as we're working.

All these leftovers.

Little bits of others.

Bones and bricks and a brooch.

I found a brooch.

And I was going to take it out but I suddenly didn't feel like it was my place.

I didn't know why it was there.

And this is his place.

And he should be here.

So I need to put something in.

Something of him.

Something to join all of that.

Something to add to the story.

So he can part of it all.

And all I have is my wedding ring.

Our ring.

The ring he chose for me to show I was his.

And I will always be his.

Only his.

But that is all I really have to give.

So I'll put that in.

I can't bury him so I will bury this.

So there is always something of him here and that everything that grows in this patch will have a bit of him in it.

She puts her ring into the ground.

An air raid siren / a plane / a lorry / an earthquake / the ground starts to shake.

Scene Three

The hydraulic fracturing stage has begun.

Bea *and* **Joseph** *are in their house.*

Joseph *is trying to mark some textbooks.*

Bea *enters. They are supposed to be having dinner so she has dressed up.*

There is a constant, almost unbearable noise from the site – a rumble, pumping, a generator hum, the kind of noise that makes it hard to think. They can hardly hear each other.

Joseph Bea, oh, you're all ready. It's nearly ready, the sauce and the veg, on the hob, I've just got this last few to do, marking, this last bit. I thought I'd be finished by now.

Bea I thought you'd be finished by now.

Joseph If I can just do these last two I can put it all away.

Bea Can I put all this away?

Joseph That's all the stuff from the meetings.

Bea Can I move it all?

Joseph I'll move it all now.

Bea Or is it all in some kind of order?

Joseph It's all in the right order, you see.

Bea Oh, Dylan drew you a picture.

It's on the top there.

Joseph (*not hearing*) What's that?

Bea It's the vegetable patch Joseph.

And that is fire in the sky.

Joseph (*distracted, not looking*) Can I look at that in a second? I just have these last ones I promise.

Bea I promise to find a day every month.

Joseph Sorry what?

Bea I'll get the wine.

Joseph I just can't think straight with all this.

Bea Red or white?

Joseph What?

Bea Red or white?

She goes to get the wine but sees that the unattended dinner is spoiling.

Joseph How are you supposed to think with all of this?

Bea   Um. Joseph. I think maybe the dinner …

Joseph *makes an exasperated sound. They cannot hear each other.*

Bea   Joseph. The water.

Joseph   It all just keeps coming . . .

Bea   The water's going everywhere.

Joseph   It's getting right in and . . .

Bea   What do you want me to do?

Joseph   Oh my God, can't they just turn it off?

Bea   Joe? Joseph.

Joseph   Turn it off. Turn it off. TURN IT OFF.

Pause. Noise.

What is that smell?

Bea *comes and sits down.*

Bea   Dinner is broken.

I'm just going to have some rice cakes.

She sits down.

They sit in the noise.

She eats out of a packet of rice cakes.

Oh, wait.

She lights the candle.

She goes and turns the light off. The room is still flooded with light from the fracking site. She turns the light switch on and off a couple of times. It makes no difference. There is just a bright harsh light that exposes everything.

Bea   It doesn't matter, we had to move our date to tonight anyway.

It's like the middle of the afternoon in here.

Joseph   We need more blackout blinds.

Bea   I'll get some more blackout blinds.

They sit in the noise. They both look around the room noticing things in the light.

Joseph   There's nowhere to hide.

Bea   This light is not kind.

Look at all the dust.

Look at all the cracks.

Joseph   Bea. Have those cracks always been there?

Bea   You're crying.

Joseph   You're crying.

Bea   I'd better go and check on Dylan.

He might be crying.

She blows the candle out and leaves.

Joseph   God, I miss being in the dark.

He throws the pile of papers from the meeting into the air. They fall.

He crumbles.

Scene Four

On the site. The day after.

*A **Geologist** is having a video call on a laptop. We don't see the other person, we only hear them. The laptop has a very distinctive cover. The **Geologist** is scrabbling around on the floor picking up pieces of paper and information they have just dropped.*

Geologist   Sorry. Sorry.

My hands are trembling.

I'm shaking in my boots here.

Big Cheese   What? This gig will be easy.

You are a Rock God.

Geologist   I'm a Geologist.

Big Cheese   Yes. You. So. Are.

And you will be fantastic. Just stick to the science. It's only a local current affairs thing. A little question-and-answer session. And have they sent you the questions already, yes? We made them do that, right? So no surprises.

Geologist   The TV crew will be here any minute.

Big Cheese   Why don't you take me through it?

Geologist   OK. Hang on.

The **Geologist** *opens another computer to face the computer we can't see.*

There.

The **Geologist** *runs a presentation infographic on the other computer.*

So I start with a short infographic showing the process so far. How far down we have drilled, then the turn horizontally right. Then it moves into where we are now.

There's the fluid going down.

Big Cheese   Wait. Go back.

Did you actually put what was on the surface?

Are those houses?

Geologist   Yes. I thought it would get everyone in mind of the scale. Put it all in perspective.

The school is on there too. And the shop.

Big Cheese   I think we should just maybe concentrate on how far down we have gone. Three thousand metres. You know that's like seven Empire State Buildings down. If you include the spire.

Geologist   Or thirty Big Bens.

Big Cheese   Exactly. Good stat.

Geologist   Or nineteen Blackpool Towers.

Big Cheese   What? Fine.

Stick to stats. Get some more ready. Throw them into the mix. Throw it at them.

How much reserve of gas there is.

How much gas is used on a daily basis.

Or or or how much energy they are using as they watch us on the one of three televisions that are on in their house, with a smartphone in their one hand and a tablet in the other, that will all need charging in the next hour, with all their lights on while cooking half of their dinner in the oven and the rest in the microwave.

Blast them with it all.

OK? Because you can't argue with figures.

Science, not scenery. OK?

Besides, if we end up drilling left next time then none of that will be of concern.

Geologist   Wouldn't that mean moving into another county?

Big Cheese   Possibly.

But it is so so so so far down. I really don't think that boundaries exist down there. Or rules.

There are no rules when it's just rocks.

Geologist   Actually there are some rules in geology and principles and laws and I'd be happy to explain some of them if you'd like to /

Big Cheese   Oh. I am so sorry. That does sound fascinating.

Utterly.

But I've got another call coming through.

Yeah. Sorry. Look. I'm going to have to go /

Geologist   But what about my run-through?

Big Cheese   Do a little practice now. On your own.

You'll be great.

OK? OK? Bye. Bye. BYEEE.

Geologist   OK.

OK

OK.

Clearing their throat, trying to find some courage.

The first question we have . . .

(*A different voice.*) The first question we have is –

There is a rumble from underground.

– is . . .

The **Fairy Queen** *suddenly appears, all guns blazing.*

Fairy Queen   What was that ear-splitting, earth-shuddering din of a THUNDERCRACK?

Geologist   Who are you?

Fairy Queen   Who are you?

Geologist   Have you been invited?

Fairy Queen   Have you?

Geologist   Are you a resident?

Fairy Queen   This is all mine.

Geologist   Oh I see. You're the owner. Hi. You're early. We're not due to start until a bit later and (*Reading*) it actually says here that your question is, 'Why don't I own the gas under my land?'

The papers are blown out of The **Geologist**'s *hand.*

Fairy Queen   Actually, I think you will find that I own everything in this field.

All that is under it.

All that is above it.

All that is on it.

Geologist   Ah. Now. Yes.

What your question is referring to there is, 'Cuius est solum eius est usque ad coelum et ad infero.' It is common thought and in common law that 'He who owns land does so up to the heavens and down to the centre of the Earth.'

Fairy Queen   He?

Geologist   Sorry. Whom ever owns the land.

And that is true up to a point. But now there are adjustments because of things like planes and airspace and in 1934 the Petroleum Act was granted that gave ownership of oil and gas to the Crown.

So we are looking for the gas but it technically belongs to the Queen.

Fairy Queen   How can it?

Geologist   She doesn't keep it. I think it is really just a way of making sure that everyone gets to use it. I think. The gas.

Fairy Queen   But I I don't know what that is and /

Geologist   Hang on, I thought the man who owned this land was a man called Keith and you're /

Fairy Queen   I. Am. The. Queen.

Geologist   Um. What?

Fairy Queen   Of the Fairies.

Geologist (*shouting*)   SECURITY.

Fairy Queen   WHY ARE YOU ALL MAKING SO MUCH NOISE?

Why are you here with all this noise and stuff and bang and BOOM?

The **Fairy Queen** *blows up the laptop.*

Geologist   Oh. OH.

But you're really tall.

Fairy Queen   How big is this *other* Queen?

Geologist   I've never actually met her.

Fairy Queen   Then why are you looking for her gas?

Geologist   I'm not looking for it for her. She just owns it.
Officially.

Gas. And oil. And coal. And silver. And gold.

Fairy Queen   She sounds like she has the right idea.

But this is still my field.

Geologist   I think maybe there are different kinds of reign.

The **Fairy Queen** *makes it rain on the* **Geologist***.*

Oh God.

Fairy Queen   What are *that*?

Geologist   That is the Work-Over Rig.

That's The Pump and Support Tower.

And that is the Gas Flare Stack.

Though the flaring off of the gas sometimes makes it look
even taller.

Fairy Queen   Explain.

Geologist   Fire. In the sky.

Fairy Queen   DRAGONS.

Geologist   There are no such things as /

Fairy Queen   Yes, there are.

And what do those words mean?

Pump-and-support tower?

Geologist   A tall metal tower that helps pump stuff into the ground.

Fairy Queen   Why?

Geologist   For the hydraulic fracturing.

A glare.

Fairy Queen   The fracturing of what?

Geologist   Um. Now. The thing is /

Fairy Queen   Of what.

Geologist   The. Ground.

Fairy Queen   My. Ground?

The **Fairy Queen** *is furious. Things are moving. A dog barks. Birds fly. The ground starts to shake and glow.*

Geologist   I can give you the name of my manager.

Because really I have absolutely no say in . . .

I am just here to look at the rocks and do presentations

And check for seismic activity and . . .

The **Geologist** *starts to read from the script in their hand.*

I, I, I understand that this might be quite a tricky and unsettling time for you and I am sorry for any inconvenience and there is an email address you can write any concerns to or there is a phone number where they'd be happy to answer any queries and if there has been any damage to property there is a special helpline . . .

The **Fairy Queen** *starts to glow red.*

Geologist   If only we could bottle that.

Scene Five

The same day. At exactly the same time.

Bea *is in the garden.*

Joseph *comes to find her.*

Joseph   He fell asleep the second he got to your mum's.

I went in with him, was just talking to your mum, we turned around and he was asleep on the floor.

Bea   I don't think he slept at all last night.

Joseph   Neither did you. I wasn't sure if you wanted to go too.

Bea   No.

Joseph   I know it would be cramped in your mum's place, but /

Bea   No.

Joseph   I could stay here. You could go. If you'd prefer that?

Bea *starts hanging up the washing.* **Joseph** *starts to hand her the pegs. It is a well-practised routine. They are silent as they do it.*

Bea   Hanging this up.

It's like we are raising little flags, isn't it?

Showing them we are still here.

Showing them we aren't going anywhere.

I'm not going anywhere.

I'm not going anywhere.

They finish hanging the washing.

Bea   Oh no. Some of this has dirt on, the, there, this one and this . . .

Oh no.

Oh.

Joseph   It's mud.

It's mud, from your fingers.

Bea   I was working on this patch before.

Joseph   You've been working so hard out here.

Bea   I thought I'd take advantage of the extra light.

Joseph   I emailed them about it.

Fifteen times.

Bea   Right.

Joseph   And wrote a letter.

Bea   OK.

Joseph   And I would have phoned but /

Bea   Yeah /

Joseph   I don't suppose you found my phone?

When you were working in here.

Because even if it doesn't work I'd like the cover.

You know?

Dylan's dinosaur sticker on the back . . .

It was here, wasn't it?

I thought it was here somewhere . . .

Just. About.

Wait. What is this?

It's a ring . . .

Bea   A ring?

Joseph   A ring-pull.

Bea   Oh.

Joseph   Now this is a proper find.

This is a round one.

An antique.

Not like they are now. All short. And square.

This is one of the round thiny massive ones.

From when we were kids.

Bea   Let me see.

Joseph   What is it?

Bea   I thought . . .

Joseph   What? What did you think?

Bea   When we started on this garden /

Joseph   When *you* started on this garden /

Bea   My mum gave me a diary my gran had written in the war.

And it was full of tips, you know, on planting and veg and and measurements and diagrams and I've been using that, for this, you know? But in amongst all of that it was full of stuff I never knew.

How she became a Land Girl. What she did after. How this all used to be fields. One big field. Our field. But after the war they built houses here. This house. That she gave us. They built houses here and she helped so that she could get one of them because she never wanted to leave this place. And how she buried her wedding ring somewhere here when she lost her husband.

And I thought maybe, maybe, just for a second, just then, that it was.

I so hoped it was a sign.

A clue.

To know what to do.

Because I look for them.

Especially on the days that I don't have one.

Like today. Like all these days.

Because I wonder what she would make of all this.

I wonder what she would do.

And I thought, you know, that was it.

Joseph   I'm sorry.

Bea   But maybe it's best it stays where it is.

Joseph   You haven't got your wedding ring on.

Bea   No. Oh no. Joseph. I didn't want to lose it.

Joseph   I don't want to lose you.

I am trying everything I can to fix this.

Bea   I know.

I know.

But that's out there. You are out there. And all I can think about is here.

I am here all the time. With this.

This is my world every day.

This is Dylan's whole world.

His world is about a mile wide. It's here. And the library. And the shop.

We know that there are bigger things, bigger places, we know it is complicated, but he doesn't know there isn't an answer to everything and he is just looking at me wondering what is going on and I'm trying and I'm trying to make it OK but it isn't, at all. All of this has arrived on our doorstep and it's knocking down the door and coming through the windows and coming up through the pipes and the noise, the noise, the noise of it and I can feel it all coming undone, I can feel it all coming apart and everything is splitting apart and it feels like everything that I was sure of, shored up by, all the foundations, everything we stood for, its all crumbling.

And I've been thinking about all that came before.

And what we had.

And what we have now.

There was a path. Down there. I used to ride my bike.

And fall off. Loads.

I used to be brave.

And I used to believe in magic.

And I don't want his world to be heavy with all of this.

We can't leave it like this.

Joseph   This isn't the end of the story.

Bea (*thinks*)   Maybe it is.

Joseph   No. Bea.

Bea   Get your phone.

Joseph   I can't.

Bea   Get my phone.

Joseph   OK.

Bea   Look up orange plants.

Joseph   Oranges grow on trees.

Bea   Look up plants with orange flowers.

Joseph   Oh. Why?

Bea   Because we are going to plant them.

Joseph (*looking on* **Bea***'s phone*)   Um . . . marigolds.

Bea   And carrots – we've already got them in.

Joseph   Dogweed midwinter.

Bea   And pumpkins.

Joseph   California poppy.

Bea   Because as next spring approached shoots started to appear.

Joseph   Only they weren't green.

Bea   They were orange. Brilliant flame orange.

Joseph   And they grew up from the ground and covered the field.

And it was said that the field itself was full of fire.

Bea   Only it won't be their fire.

It will be ours.

This is our place.

This is still our place.

This is a good place.

We have been in a good place and it will be again.

But there will be dark.

There will always be dark.

And there will be too much noise, and too little, and there will be cracks and leaks and loss and battles and wins and things we can't do anything about other than hang fast and try and stand our ground because this is a good place.

This is an old place. This is our place.

This is their place. Whoever came before.

And all we need to do is soak it up.

Isn't it?

Because it must have gone somewhere, mustn't it?

All that comes out of us.

All that comes out of them.

All that came before.

The love and laughter and the life and the sweat and the tears and the blood and the hope and the cross and the pain and the loss and the brave and the words must be what we stand on and must be hanging in the air.

And we have to think about what we put into it all.

And I need to make sure this is a good place again.

I am made of the same stuff.

Because now it's my turn to be in charge.

Because it's time to take our turn.

And we just have to hold on.

Make sure we give it all back.

And until it is our winter,

This is our watch.

And we just have to hold tight.

The ground starts to shake and fall apart and there is noise and music and time and light and everything that has come before swirls all around them. They hold on to each other as everything else falls apart.

Scene Six

The future. An archaeological dig. The same area marked off by string and wooden stakes. An **Archaeologist** *and a* **Volunteer** *are carefully brushing the ground off a big find. They are uncovering all kinds of devices – a 1980s TV, iPhones, laptops, a Betamax, amidst dust and earth and plastic bags and plastic tat and a printer and wires and cables.*

Archaeologist   It is. IT IS. I mean this is just . . . If this is . . .

Volunteer   Is it?

Archaeologist   Careful. Careful.

Volunteer   It is, isn't it?

Archaeologist   Yes. Yes. What you are looking at here is a totally intact SL-8080UB Betamax video recorder. Some slight oxidation but it will clean up.

Volunteer   I don't believe it.

Archaeologist   AND IT IS SECURITY MARKED.

You must be my lucky charm.

Volunteer   Wait, what's under /

Archaeologist   That. That is a Triniton Television.

They are often found in pairs but they are not often found.

This is just . . . just . . . .

Volunteer   And more.

Archaeologist   An iPhone 3

An iPhone 6

This one has a cracked screen.

Volunteer   Ah yes. A common ailment of the era.

Archaeologist   And and and a picture of a dinosaur on the back.

Volunteer   Wondrous.

Archaeologist   An iPhone 10.

An iPhone 27.

Volunteer   Is that not an Apple Watch?

Archaeologist   Great spot.

That is a later version, as it is so small.

Volunteer   Laptop computers here.

(*It is the* **Geologist***'s laptop.*)

Volunteer   PLASTIC BAGS.

Archaeologist   A finding of this scale . . .

Volunteer   SOFT. DRINKS. CANS.

With ring-pulls attached.

Archaeologist   It can only mean one thing.

What we have stumbled across here is Screen Age.

It is a Screen Age. Land. Fill. Site.

Volunteer   No.

Archaeologist   What we are looking at here is a hoard from around the time of THE POWER CUTS but it predates the beginning of the Second Dark Age.

Incredible.

That is a ZX SPECTRUM.

Volunteer   They must have had rooms just full of stuff.

And what is that there, what is that, down there, under there/

Archaeologist   A. cassette. player.

And its plug.

Volunteer   How did it work?

Archaeologist (*trying to connect the power cable*)   This bit must have gone here. No here.

There.

Volunteer   Can I hold it?

The **Archaeologist** *proudly gives it over. The* **Volunteer** *takes it and beams.*

Pause.

The **Volunteer** *inspects the cassette player then holds up the plug.*

Volunteer   So what went into here?

End.

DRAMA ONLINE

A new way to study drama

From curriculum classics
to contemporary writing
Accompanied by
theory and practice

Discover. Read. Study. Perform.

Find out more:
www.dramaonlinelibrary.com

 FOLLOW US ON TWITTER @DRAMAONLINELIB

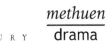

Bloomsbury Methuen Drama Modern Plays

include work by

Bola Agbaje
Edward Albee
Davey Anderson
Jean Anouilh
John Arden
Peter Barnes
Sebastian Barry
Alistair Beaton
Brendan Behan
Edward Bond
William Boyd
Bertolt Brecht
Howard Brenton
Amelia Bullmore
Anthony Burgess
Leo Butler
Jim Cartwright
Lolita Chakrabarti
Caryl Churchill
Lucinda Coxon
Curious Directive
Nick Darke
Shelagh Delaney
Ishy Din
Claire Dowie
David Edgar
David Eldridge
Dario Fo
Michael Frayn
John Godber
Paul Godfrey
James Graham
David Greig
John Guare
Mark Haddon
Peter Handke
David Harrower
Jonathan Harvey
Iain Heggie

Robert Holman
Caroline Horton
Terry Johnson
Sarah Kane
Barrie Keeffe
Doug Lucie
Anders Lustgarten
David Mamet
Patrick Marber
Martin McDonagh
Arthur Miller
D. C. Moore
Tom Murphy
Phyllis Nagy
Anthony Neilson
Peter Nichols
Joe Orton
Joe Penhall
Luigi Pirandello
Stephen Poliakoff
Lucy Prebble
Peter Quilter
Mark Ravenhill
Philip Ridley
Willy Russell
Jean-Paul Sartre
Sam Shepard
Martin Sherman
Wole Soyinka
Simon Stephens
Peter Straughan
Kate Tempest
Theatre Workshop
Judy Upton
Timberlake Wertenbaker
Roy Williams
Snoo Wilson
Frances Ya-Chu Cowhig
Benjamin Zephaniah

Bloomsbury Methuen Drama Contemporary Dramatists

include

John Arden (two volumes)
Arden & D'Arcy
Peter Barnes (three volumes)
Sebastian Barry
Mike Bartlett
Dermot Bolger
Edward Bond (eight volumes)
Howard Brenton (two volumes)
Leo Butler
Richard Cameron
Jim Cartwright
Caryl Churchill (two volumes)
Complicite
Sarah Daniels (two volumes)
Nick Darke
David Edgar (three volumes)
David Eldridge (two volumes)
Ben Elton
Per Olov Enquist
Dario Fo (two volumes)
Michael Frayn (four volumes)
John Godber (four volumes)
Paul Godfrey
James Graham
David Greig
John Guare
Lee Hall (two volumes)
Katori Hall
Peter Handke
Jonathan Harvey (two volumes)
Iain Heggie
Israel Horovitz
Declan Hughes
Terry Johnson (three volumes)
Sarah Kane
Barrie Keeffe
Bernard-Marie Koltès (two volumes)
Franz Xaver Kroetz
Kwame Kwei-Armah
David Lan
Bryony Lavery
Deborah Levy
Doug Lucie

David Mamet (four volumes)
Patrick Marber
Martin McDonagh
Duncan McLean
David Mercer (two volumes)
Anthony Minghella (two volumes)
Tom Murphy (six volumes)
Phyllis Nagy
Anthony Neilson (two volumes)
Peter Nichol (two volumes)
Philip Osment
Gary Owen
Louise Page
Stewart Parker (two volumes)
Joe Penhall (two volumes)
Stephen Poliakoff (three volumes)
David Rabe (two volumes)
Mark Ravenhill (three volumes)
Christina Reid
Philip Ridley (two volumes)
Willy Russell
Eric-Emmanuel Schmitt
Ntozake Shange
Sam Shepard (two volumes)
Martin Sherman (two volumes)
Christopher Shinn
Joshua Sobel
Wole Soyinka (two volumes)
Simon Stephens (three volumes)
Shelagh Stephenson
David Storey (three volumes)
C. P. Taylor
Sue Townsend
Judy Upton
Michel Vinaver (two volumes)
Arnold Wesker (two volumes)
Peter Whelan
Michael Wilcox
Roy Williams (four volumes)
David Williamson
Snoo Wilson (two volumes)
David Wood (two volumes)
Victoria Wood

Bloomsbury Methuen Drama Student Editions

Jean Anouilh *Antigone* • John Arden *Serjeant Musgrave's Dance* • Alan Ayckbourn *Confusions* • Aphra Behn *The Rover* • Edward Bond *Lear* • *Saved* • Bertolt Brecht *The Caucasian Chalk Circle* • *Fear and Misery in the Third Reich* • *The Good Person of Szechwan* • *Life of Galileo* • *Mother Courage and Her Children* • *The Resistible Rise of Arturo Ui* • *The Threepenny Opera* • Anton Chekhov *The Cherry Orchard* • *The Seagull* • *Three Sisters* • *Uncle Vanya* • Caryl Churchill *Serious Money* • *Top Girls* • Shelagh Delaney *A Taste of Honey* • Euripides *Elektra* • *Medea* • Dario Fo *Accidental Death of an Anarchist* • Michael Frayn *Copenhagen* • John Galsworthy *Strife* • Nikolai Gogol *The Government Inspector* • Carlo Goldoni *A Servant to Two Masters* • Lorraine Hansberry *A Raisin in the Sun* • Robert Holman *Across Oka* • Henrik Ibsen *A Doll's House* • *Ghosts* • *Hedda Gabler* • Sarah Kane *4.48 Psychosis* • *Blasted* • Charlotte Keatley *My Mother Said I Never Should* • Bernard Kops *Dreams of Anne Frank* • Federico García Lorca *Blood Wedding* • *Doña Rosita the Spinster* (bilingual edition) • *The House of Bernarda Alba* (bilingual edition) • *Yerma* (bilingual edition) • David Mamet *Glengarry Glen Ross* • *Oleanna* • Patrick Marber *Closer* • John Marston *The Malcontent* • Martin McDonagh *The Lieutenant of Inishmore* • *The Lonesome West* • *The Beauty Queen of Leenane* • Arthur Miller *All My Sons* • *The Crucible* • *A View from the Bridge* • *Death of a Salesman* • *The Price* • *After the Fall* • *The Last Yankee* • *A Memory of Two Mondays* • *Broken Glass* • Joe Orton *Loot* • Joe Penhall *Blue/Orange* • Luigi Pirandello *Six Characters in Search of an Author* • Lucy Prebble *Enron* • Mark Ravenhill *Shopping and F***ing* • Willy Russell *Blood Brothers* • *Educating Rita* • Sophocles *Antigone* • *Oedipus the King* • Wole Soyinka *Death and the King's Horseman* • Shelagh Stephenson *The Memory of Water* • August Strindberg *Miss Julie* • J. M. Synge *The Playboy of the Western World* • Theatre Workshop *Oh What a Lovely War* • Frank Wedekind *Spring Awakening* • Timberlake Wertenbaker *Our Country's Good* • Arnold Wesker *The Merchant* • Oscar Wilde *The Importance of Being Earnest* • Tennessee Williams *A Streetcar Named Desire* • *The Glass Menagerie* • *Cat on a Hot Tin Roof* • *Sweet Bird of Youth*

Bloomsbury Methuen Drama World Classics
include

Jean Anouilh (two volumes)
John Arden (two volumes)
Brendan Behan
Aphra Behn
Bertolt Brecht (eight volumes)
Georg Büchner
Mikhail Bulgakov
Pedro Calderón
Karel Čapek
Peter Nichols (two volumes)
Anton Chekhov
Noël Coward (eight volumes)
Georges Feydeau (two volumes)
Eduardo De Filippo
Max Frisch (two volumes)
John Galsworthy
Nikolai Gogol (two volumes)
Maxim Gorky (two volumes)
Harley Granville Barker
(two volumes)
Victor Hugo
Henrik Ibsen (six volumes)

Alfred Jarry
Federico García Lorca
(three volumes)
Pierre Marivaux
Mustapha Matura
David Mercer
(two volumes)
Arthur Miller (six volumes)
Molière
Pierre de Musset
Joe Orton
A. W. Pinero
Luigi Pirandello
Terence Rattigan
W. Somerset Maugham
August Strindberg
(three volumes)
J. M. Synge
Ramón del Valle-Inclán
Frank Wedekind
Oscar Wilde
Tennessee Williams

For a complete listing of Bloomsbury
Methuen Drama titles, visit:

www.bloomsbury.com/drama

Follow us on Twitter and keep up to date
with our news and publications

@MethuenDrama

CPSIA information can be obtained
at www.ICGtesting.com
Printed in the USA
LVOW04s2102080616

491778LV00012B/147/P